# The Dalmatian

A Complete and Comprehensive Owners
Guide to: Buying, Owning, Health,
Grooming, Training, Obedience,
Understanding and Caring for Your
Dalmatian

## Michael Stonewood

ISBN: 9781091967519

# The Dalmatian

# CONTENTS

# INTRODUCTION

Before purchasing any pet it is important to understand that as a pet owner you are responsible for the care and wellbeing of your pet. It is important to try and learn as much as you can about the animal you are considering to keep as a pet to make sure that your lifestyle, household and financial status are suited to provide your pet with the best possible care. This guide has been designed to provide you with both precise and concise information about a Dalmatian's basic needs to help you provide your pet with the best quality care practices. This guide will give an in-depth explanation on training your Dalmatian, raising your Dalmatian from a puppy, grooming, health care and everything in between!

# DESCRIPTION

The Dalmatian is a large breed of dog that originates from Croatia. The breed is most noted for its highly unique black, or liver, spotted coat which has earned the breed the nicknames of 'Plum Pudding Dog' and the 'Leopard Carriage Dog.' Despite the breed originating from Croatia, the Dalmatian was mainly developed and cultivated in the United Kingdom. In 1890 the United Kingdom was the first country to actually have an official Dalmatian club and breed standard. The Dalmatian were originally used for a plethora of different tasks: as dogs of war, as guard dogs and as companion dogs. The modern day Dalmatian still has a high instinct to guard its owners and will be friendly and loyal to people it knows but often aloof with strangers and unknown dogs. In the early 1900s, the Dalmatian started to be used in sporting hunts as was used as a bird dog, trail hound, a retriever and in packs to hunt wild boar or stags. It was discovered that Dalmatians and horses are very compatible, and the Dalmatian soon was used to run in front of horse drawn carriages to clear a path for the horses. As the breed's large amount of working roles suggests, the Dalmatian is a highly adaptable and intelligent breed that is capable of being trained to do nearly any job. The Dalmatian is born with a solid white coat and they slowly develop

their characteristic spots at around 3 to 4 weeks old -
after about a month or two they have developed most
of their spots. Most Dalmatian are born with a smooth
short coat that sheds continuously throughout the year.
However it is not uncommon for a Dalmatian to be born
with a long haired coat – interestingly the long haired
Dalmatians shed considerably less than their short
haired counterparts. As a whole the Dalmatian is a
highly intelligent and affectionate breed that thrives
both in working environments and household
environments. It is important to well socialize your
Dalmatian during its puppyhood to make it less
suspicious and aloof with strangers and unknown dogs.

## Lifespan

A Dalmatian will normally live to be between 12
and 14 years old. However it is not uncommon for a
Dalmatian to live to be as old as 16, providing that it
does not develop any serious health issues.

## Height and Weight

A fully grown Dalmatian will normally stand
between 19 to 24 inches (48.25 to 61cm) tall at the
shoulder. A healthy adult Dalmatian will normally weigh
between 48 to 55 pounds (21.75 to 25kg). It is important
to note that the weight of a healthy Dalmatian depends

on how large the Dalmatian is – taller Dalmatian should weigh more.

# BREED CHARACTERISTICS

The following section will give you a simplistic overview of the characteristics of a Dalmatian. Our rating system is from 1 to 10 – with 1 being the lowest score and 10 being the highest.

- ➢ **Adaptability:** 6/10
- ➢ **Friendliness:** 8/10
- ➢ **Health:** 8/10
- ➢ **Ease of Grooming:** 10/10
- ➢ **Amount of Shedding:** 10/10
- ➢ **Trainability:** 6/10
- ➢ **Intelligence:** 8/10
- ➢ **Exercise Needed:** 10/10
- ➢ **Playfulness:** 8/10
- ➢ **Family Friendliness:** 10/10

# WHY SHOULD YOU PURCHASE A DOG?

In the United States of America it is estimated that there are between 70 and 80 million pet dogs owned and over 40% of the county's households own a dog! As the statistic shows dogs are incredibly popular pets – but why? Any dog owner will happily tell you all the benefits and joys of owning a dog! The following section will outline 5 key benefits of owning a dog:

## Companionship

Dogs are incredibly loyal and loving animals and make a great addition to any household. If you build a strong relationship with your pet they can transcend just being a pet and become a friend, or ever a member of your family! However your dog brings you companionship in other ways. You are more likely to interact with strangers while walking your dog than if you were walking alone. Owning a dog also allows you to go to dog parks and converse with other dog owners. If you walk your dog around your neighborhood on a regular basis, you may also develop a friendly relationship with your neighbors who own dogs as you are likely to pass each other several times a day.

## Exercise

Owning a dog increases your chance of exercising due to the fact that you will need to play with and walk your dog. Taking your pet for frequent walks will decrease your chance of becoming over weight. A recent study in Australia found that children with a pet dog are 50% less likely to be overweight! Exercising on a regular basis has a plethora of other health benefits such as reducing the chance of heart disease, strokes and high blood pressure. A dog can be a great exercise companion as well as being a great motivation due to the fact that it is cruel to not provide your dog with adequate exercise.

## Watchdog

Dogs are very territorial, loyal and aware as a species. Even from as early as puppyhood, a dog is able to detect potential burglars and dangers. Your dog will bark at anything suspicious or out of the ordinary which will alert you to any potential trouble. Most criminals are instantly put off by the barking of a watchdog.

## Nurturing

The majority of humans have a deep desire to nurture. This desire used to be fulfilled by caring for, and raising, a baby or caring for younger siblings. Across the Western World the average family size is decreasing which makes pets the perfect outlet for people's nurturing desires. In families with no children, or one child, dogs are fulfilling the role of being substitute children and siblings! Dogs are intelligent beings and respond well to being nurtured which makes it a positive and rewarding experiences for both the owner and the pet. Dogs also seem to nurture children. Children who own a dog tend to have a high self-esteem and are more popular with their classmates!

## Empathy

Dogs are incredibly empathetic animals! They will sense the mood of their owner and either attempt to provide comfort, through physical contact, or a distraction through a humorous playful act. It is not uncommon for dogs to bring their distressed owners their favorite toy as an attempt to cheer them up. Dogs have also saved their owners from countless dangers – such as house fires and burglaries.

## Responsibility

Purchasing a dog is one of the best ways to teach young children about the concept of responsibility. If you purchase a dog for your family and allow a child to be involved with caring for the dog it will help them to develop selflessness and responsibility. A child can be tasked with simple care routines such as: changing the water in the dog's bowl, feeding the dog or giving the dog its treats during training. If your child is older, or already has a good understanding of responsibility, you can give them more complex care tasks such as: grooming the dog, training the dog or walking the dog. Older children can also be given the task of introducing their younger siblings to the process of playing with and caring for a new dog.

# DOG EQUIPMENT BASICS AND ESSENTIALS

Before purchasing a Dalmatian it is important to make sure that you have already purchased all the equipment you will need to provide your new Dalmatian with the best possible care. Ensuring you have all the essential equipment before purchasing your pet is the best way to build a strong relationship with your pet and to keep it content, happy and healthy.

## Collars and ID Tags

Purchasing a collar with an ID tag is arguably one of the most important things you can purchase for your Dalmatian. The collar allows you to attach a leash to your Dalmatian, which in turns allows you to take your pet for a walk which is essential to their health. There are a wide range of collars available to purchase made from multiple different materials and styles. It is important to take your dog's habits into account when purchasing a collar. For example if your dog regularly enjoys swimming it is not advisable to purchase a leather collar. It is also important to not purchase a thin collar! When you walk your Dalmatian on a leash it may lunge, or pull, which will cause the collar to dig into its neck. The wider the collar is the wider the area the force from the lunge is spread over – basically wider collars are more comfortable! The ID tag allows for your pet to be easily identifiable and returned to you if they are ever lost! I recommend having your Dalmatian's name and your home address on the ID tag. This will allow the person who finds your dog to keep it calm by using its familiar name and will know where to return your pet to.

## Leashes and Harnesses

Purchasing a lead, or harness, is vital in ensuring your Dalmatian remains healthy! Having a lead, or harness, allows for you to walk your pet and provide them with the exercise they need. Walking your pet also helps to create a strong bond and friendship between the two of you. There are a few differences between Leashes and Harnesses which will be explained below:

> ➢ **Leash:** Most dog owners will use a leash while walking their pet. Leashes ensure both comfort and safety when you take your dog out for a walk. It is important to buy a leash that extends to allow your dog to explore and move away from you at times. It is equally important to buy a sturdy leash that will allow you to keep control of your pet for the entirety of the walk.

> **Harness:** If you have a large, small, energetic or boisterous dog a harness may be a safer option. The harness is safer for these types of dogs as they will not feel discomfort from their collar when they pull against the leash. Purchasing a front-clip harness (that goes over the dog's chest) will allow you to have more control over your pet.

## Bedding

Some owners allow their dogs to sleep in their beds or on their sofas. While this can definitely be a great way to build a strong relationship with your dog it is also important to purchase a suitable bed for your pet. By providing your pet with its own bed it will give your dog a place of its own to feel safe and secure. There is an overwhelmingly wide variety of dog beds available in pet stores and on the internet. I recommend adhering to the following criteria when purchasing a dog bed to ensure both practicality, safety, comfort and warmth.

> **Natural Materials:** It is important to make sure the dog bed you purchase is made of natural materials. Synthetic products, including fire retardant and stain-proof chemicals, may be harmful to your dog's health.

➢ **Removable Cover:** If you purchase a dog bed that has a removable cover it allows for you to regularly and easily clean your dog's bed. Keeping your pet's bedding clean is essential to keeping your pet healthy as it removes bacteria and any parasites that may have found their way into the bedding. Purchasing a bed with a removable cover also allows you to replace the cover if it keeps overly worn and ripped – replacing just the cover is a lot less expensive than replacing an entire bed!

➢ **Non-Skid Bottom:** When your dog dives into its bed you do not want it to slide across the floor as this could cause damage to your pet, the bed and the floor. Purchasing a bed with a non-skid bottom removes the chance of injury and damages.

➢ **Plan Ahead:** If you are buying a puppy it is important to remember that your puppy will grow! It is considered best practice to purchase a bed that is the correct size for an adult dog so it will not be out grown.

There are two main categories of beds that are suitable for dogs. It is important to watch your dog sleep so you have an idea of how its sleeping preferences and how it physically lies down. Choosing the correct bedding is vital to ensure your dog feels safe and secure at home. The two categories of bedding are as follows:

> ➢ **Round / Nest-Style Beds:** These beds are ideal for smaller dogs and larger dogs who like to curl up when they sleep.
> ➢ **Raised / Cushion / Futon Beds:** These beds are ideal for dogs who enjoy stretching themselves out when they sleep.

## Food and Water Bowls

It is important to purchase a food bowl and a water bowl for your pet Dalmatian. There are three main materials that are used to create these bowls: plastic, ceramic, stainless steel. The following section will outline the pros and cons of each material.

> ➢ **Plastic:** Plastic bowls are cheap, durable and long lasting. The only downside of a plastic bowl is that plastic can be toxic to dogs if ingested. If you notice your dog gnawing at its bowl you should replace it with either a ceramic or stainless steel bowl.
> ➢ **Ceramic:** Ceramic bowls are very stable and heavy which makes them a good choice if your dog pushes its bowl while it eats or drinks. The main downside of using a ceramic

bowl is that they are porous and will therefore need to be thoroughly cleaned on a daily basis.

➢ **Stainless Steel:** Stainless Steel bowls are recommended by vets and dog care experts. They are easy to clean, easy to sanitize, durable and inexpensive. Similar to when purchasing a dog bed, it is considered best practice to purchase a stainless steel bowl with a non-skid bottom to prevent the bowl from moving while your dog eats or drinks.

## Worms, Ticks and Fleas

Part of your responsibility as a Dalmatian owner is to control and kill the parasites that your Dalmatian will definitely get at some point. Worms, Ticks and Fleas can cause serious discomfort and health issues if left unchecked. There are medicated collars and shampoos that help to minimize your Dalmatian's chance of getting fleas and ticks. There are also medicines you can purchase to help prevent both external and internal parasites. It is considered best practice to take your pet to your local vet and ask for them to give you a prescription for medicines to control parasites.

## Toys

Toys for your Dalmatian are essential for so many different reasons! Toys can provide your pet with mental and physical stimulation which can also lead them to having less destructive behavior patterns – such as chewing up furniture! Chew toys can also have dental health benefits. Toys also allow you to build a strong and fun relationship with your pet. The following list details some of the most popular toys available on the market:

> ➢ **Chew Toys:** Chew toys can provide your dog with hours of solo fun and can also help your dog to develop a strong and healthy jaw. Before giving your dog a chew toy it is important to check that it is not too hard – an overly hard chew toy can have the opposite effect and damage your dog's jaw! A good rule of thumb is to bang the chew toy on your knee – if it hurts it is too hard for your dog's mouth! It is likewise important to make sure that your dog does not ingest any of the chew toy though as the plastic, or rubber, is toxic!
> ➢ **Tug Toys:** Tug toys are a very popular choice as they allow for you to actively play with your dog. It is important to not allow your dog to become aggressive while you play

with the tug toy! To avoid your dog becoming aggressive you should keep a positive and happy inflexion in your voice. The most popular choices for tug toys are ropes and squishy plastic bones.

➢ **Balls and Fetch Toys:** Balls and fetch toys are another great way to actively play with your pet. It is important to purchase fetch toys made of soft plastic so your dog will suffer no dental damage or physical pain (if they miss the catch and get hit by the toy). A good choice for fetch toys are ball, Frisbees, cuddly toys and squishy plastic sticks. Tennis balls are a common choice for fetch but are not actually a healthy choice of toy! The covering on Tennis balls can actually abrade the enamel on your dog's teeth which can lead to serious health, and dental, issues in later life.

➢ **Food-Dispensing Toys:** Food-dispensing toys are a great way to mentally stimulate your dog. They come in a variety of different styles and shapes. I recommended purchasing a ball or cube as it will also allow your dog to push the toy around which encourages physical activity as well.

## Expanding your Collection

Dogs are incredibly intelligent beings and, like humans, have preferences when it comes to bedding, food and how they have fun. Once you have developed a good understanding of your new Dalmatian's preferences I recommended taking these preferences into account when purchasing new equipment and food.

# BASIC COST OF OWNING A DOG

Owning a dog obviously costs money – but how much money? The following section will provide you with the average cost of owning a dog to help you decide whether you are in the correct financial state and to help you budget for any unexpected bills! It is important to remember that on average, dogs live for between 8 and 18 years.

## Initial costs

- ➢ **Purchase of Dog:** Most Dalmatian breeds cost between $200 and $1500.
- ➢ **Microchip:** If your Dalmatian has not been microchipped before purchase this will cost $50.
- ➢ **Lifetime Council Registration:** This costs $49 for desexed Dalmatian and $182 for Dalmatian who have not been desexed.

## Basic Equipment

- ➢ **Dog Bed:** Dog beds normally cost between $20 and $200.
- ➢ **Brush:** Most brushes designed for grooming cost around $20.

- ➢ **Food and Water bowls:** Each bowl costs are $20 and you will need a minimum of two – one for water and one for food.
- ➢ **Collar, Lead, Tags and Harnesses:** A complete set will normally cost between $50 and $200.
- ➢ **Toys:** Dogs need a range of toys. I recommend setting aside between $50 and $100 dollars to provide your dog with the enough toys.

## Preventative Health Care

- ➢ **Vaccination:** Vaccinations cost between $50 and $120 depending on which ones you get. Your dog will need vaccine at 8, 12 and 16 weeks of age and then every 3 years after that.
- ➢ **Worm Tablets:** Tapeworm and Heartworm prevention tablets cost about $10 a month.
- ➢ **Fleas:** Most flea prevention cost around $10 a month.
- ➢ **Bi-annual Vet Check:** You will need to take your dog for a health check at the vet every 6 months. A general health checkup costs around $65.

## Food

- **Basic Food Needs:** Basic food (kibble) will cost you around $1,200 a year.
- **Treats:** Treats are not essential but most owners enjoy giving them to their dogs. I recommend budgeting around $100 a year for dog treats.
- **Dental Chew Sticks:** Dental chew sticks are a great way to improve your dog's jaw strength and dental hygiene. I recommend budgeting around $100 a year for dental chew sticks.

## Grooming

- **Shampoo and Conditioner:** Shampoo and conditioner will normally cost around $30 a year. It is not necessary to buy expensive brands of shampoo and condition – basic products designed for dogs will work perfectly fine.
- **Visit to the Groomer:** Groomers normally charge between $50 and $150. I recommend taking your dog to the groomers at least twice a year.

## Training, Dog Care and Walking

> **Puppy Training:** Puppy training normally costs around $100 for a month long training course.
> **Advanced Training:** Most owners enjoy taking their dogs to obedience classes and advanced training. These services normally cost around $170 for a month long course.
> **Dog Walking:** Dog walking normally costs around $25 an hour (depending on where you live).
> **Daycare:** Daycare services normally cost around $50 a day.
> **Boarding:** I recommend budgeting around $300 a year on boarding services. Most boarding services will charge around $50 a day.

## Other Expenses

While I would love to tell you that the expenses listed above are the only expense you will incur while owning a dog, it is far from the truth. Dogs, like small children, are energetic, curious and playful. This can lead your pet to causing unexpected damages to furniture, your home and your car. All puppies will at some point destroy something valuable. When introducing a new dog into your home, I highly suggest moving your valuables into a safe, and out of reach, place. For example, if you have a recently added a large dog breed to your home it might be worthwhile removing the expensive vase you have as a table center piece until you know your dog will not disturb it. Likewise, if you have recently added a small dog to your home it might be worthwhile ensuring there are no small holes for your dog to climb inside. You do not want a small dog to get stuck in a small hole and end up having to damage your property to rescue your pet. When it comes to new dogs, it is always better to air on the side of caution! Puppies are known to chew anything they can get their mouth around, this includes: your television remote, laptop chargers, the gear stick in your car and the list goes on and on. I urge you to take preventative measures and protect your valuable possessions while your new pet settles into your home.

# PURCHASING YOUR NEW PET

There are multiple different ways to purchase a dog: from a breeder, from a pet store or from a rescue service. There are pros and cons of each method and they will be explained in the following section.

## Breeders

When it comes to purchasing a Dalmatian, breeders are unarguably the best method. A breeder will allow you to interact with your Dalmatian before you purchase it. This will allow you to understand the Dalmatian temperament and behavior as well as allowing you to inspect the Dalmatian for any genetic defects. Breeders are normally a part of a registered service – such as The Kennel Club. By being a member of a registered organization it gives the breeder accountability and legitimacy. Breeders will be able to inform you of any issues with the Dalmatian and how they have been socializing it. Breeders will also be able to tell you the exact birthdate of your new Dalmatian. The only downside of breeders is the fact that they are more expensive than pet stores – however this should not be an issue when you are considering purchasing a Dalmatian.

## Pet Stores

Pet stores are a common choice when purchasing a
new Dalmatian – but I HIGHLY do not recommend
purchasing a Dalmatian from a pet store! Most pet
stores purchase their Dalmatian from puppy mills. Puppy
mills are notorious for breeding and raising their
Dalmatian in terrible conditions which leads to both
behavioral and health problems. Employees at the pet
store will most likely not be able to provide you with
specific information about a Dalmatian – they are
unlikely to know its exact date of birth and health
background. The pedigree of a Dalmatian from a pet
store is also questionable. Pet stores have a terrible
return policy! It is not uncommon for a new owner to
not have fully considered every aspect of owning a
Dalmatian and they therefore return it. If you return a
Dalmatian to a breeder you can be assured that the
Dalmatian will lead a happy life. However, if you return a
Dalmatian to a pet store it will most likely be
euthanized, if it has grown to be older than a puppy, due
to the fact that it is unlikely to sell.

## Rescue

If you are an experienced Dalmatian owner you
may considered getting a Dalmatian from a rescue
shelter. Most Dalmatian from rescue shelters are free

and the shelter just wishes you to make a donation. It is important to remember that rescue Dalmatian may have health or behavioral issues due to their turbulent lives. Dalmatian in rescue shelters are also hardly ever puppies and tend to be middle aged or older. However by getting your Dalmatian from a rescue shelter allows you to give a Dalmatian a better life than they would have had in the past. Most Dalmatian that end up in shelters have been cruelly treated or abandoned and by adopting one you are giving the animal a chance to experience life in a loving home.

# PUPPY CARE

When purchasing a Dalmatian both first time owners and veteran owners normally opt for buying a puppy. Purchasing a puppy will allow you to establish a good and healthy relationship with your dog and will set the foundation for a long happy friendship. Another reason puppies are so popular is due to the fact that they are among some of the most adorable creatures on the planet! However caring for a new puppy is not the easiest thing. You will have to be prepared to make some huge lifestyles changes to accommodate your new puppy. The following section is a simple and concise guide to help you care for the new canine addition to your family.

## Find a Good Vet

Before purchasing your puppy it is a good idea to research the vets in your local area. It is very important to find a vet that is local and highly qualified. The best way to find a good vet is by asking your friends, local dog walkers, local dog groomers, asking the breeder and researching online. Once you purchase your new puppy you should take it straight to your vet for a checkup. The checkup visit will make sure that your puppy is in good health and free from any serious birth defects or genetic health issues. Introducing your vet to your new Dalmatian while it is young also allows for your puppy to become familiar with the vet – this can help avoid stress during later visits. By taking your puppy to the vet straight away, it also allows you to start a health care routine with your pet. It is important to set up a vaccination plan with your vet and also to discuss the best methods for control parasites (both internal and external).

## Food

It is important to purchase food that is formulated specifically for puppies. A decent brand will have a statement from the Association of American Feed Control Officials (AAFCO), or your countries equivalent, on the packaging to ensure that the food you are purchasing is going to fulfil your puppy's nutritional requirements. Small and medium-sized breeds can start eating adult dog food when they are between 9 and 12 months of age. Larger breeds of dog should be fed on puppy kibbles until they reach 2 years of age. It is important to make sure that your puppy has cool, fresh and clean water available to them at all times.

## Feeding Schedule

Puppies have a different feeding schedule to adult

dogs. Their feeding schedule changes as they get older. I recommend feeding your puppy on the following schedule:

- ➤ **6 – 12 weeks old:** 4 meals per day
- ➤ **3 – 6 months old:** 3 meals per day
- ➤ **6 – 12 months old:** 2 meals per day

## Obedience Training

It is important to train your new puppy to be obedient. Obedience will allow your puppy to have a life full of positive interactions as well as forging a stronger bond between you and your pet. It is important to teach your puppy simple commands such as sit, stay, down and come. These commands will help to keep your dog safe and under control in any potentially dangerous situations. I recommend attending a local obedience training class. Obedience classes allow for you and your dog to learn the best methods for each process and command. Obedience classes also allow you, and your puppy, to interact with other people and dogs of all ages and from all backgrounds. It is important to remember that positive reinforcement has been proven to be a dramatically more effective process than punishment.

## Bathroom Training

Housetraining is a priority if you want to keep your house clean! Before you start your housetraining it is important to locate a suitable location for your puppy to go to the bathroom. If your puppy has not had all of its vaccinations it is important to find a bathroom that is inaccessible to other animals. This will help to avoid your puppy getting any unnecessary viruses or diseases. There are three key tricks to keep in mind when you are attempting to housetrain your puppy: positive reinforcement, planning and patience. It is important positively praise your puppy when they go to the bathroom outside and not to punish them when inevitable accidents will happen. I recommend the following times to try and introduce your puppy to a bathroom routine:

➢ When you first wake up.
➢ When your puppy wakes up from any naps it might have.
➢ During and after physical exercise.
➢ After your puppy eats or drinks a lot of water.
➢ Immediately before bed time.

## Be Social

The main way to avoid your puppy developing behavioral problems is to be social with it. At approximately 2 to 4 months old, most puppies will begin to accept other animals, people, places and experiences. It is important to start socializing your puppy with as many people and animals as possible. I recommend bringing your puppy to a dog park, to your friends or relatives houses, to dog friendly restaurants and to have other people accompany you while you walk your pet. By interacting with multiple different types of people and animals your puppy will learn to be more social and accepting.

## Signs of Illness

It is important to watch your puppy closely to make sure that it is not exhibiting any signs of illness. Your puppy is at its most vulnerable stage of its development while also being at its most important stage of development. If you notice any of the following signs you should take your puppy to the vet immediately: lack of appetite, vomiting, lack of weight gain, lack of growth, diarrhea, pale gums, nasal discharge, inability to pass urine and stool, lethargy, swelling and difficulty breathing.

## Spaying and Neutering

There are a lot of factors to considered when deciding if you should spay or neuter your puppy. Many owners refuse to spay or neuter their puppy due to the fact that they find it morally wrong and unnatural. However most owners do decide to have their pet neutered. Shelter euthanasia is the number one killer of dogs and companion animals throughout America. In Atlanta alone over 15 million dollars is spent annually on euthanizing unwanted dogs! The only way to avoid this is to have your pet spayed or neutered. Dogs face some discomfort if they are in heat or are unable to mate. Spaying and neutering creates no long term health problems for your pet. At the end of the day it is an important decision for you and your family to make. I advise talking it over with your vet and family/friends who have already been through the process.

# DOG CARE

Once your puppy has grown up, or if you have purchased an adult Dalmatian, you will need to change how you care for it.

## Dog Food

There are so many different brands of dog food available: organic, all natural, hypo-allergenic, vegetarian and even vegan! Good dog food is vital to provide your pet with the nutrition it needs to reach its full potential both physically and mentally. Good nutrition helps your Dalmatian fight disease, prevents obesity, minimizes your dog's chance of getting an illness and generally improves your Dalmatian's overall health and happiness. It is important to remember that the advertising on dog food is aimed at humans – because I are the ones that pay for it! You should only feed your dog food that has been approved by the Association of American Feed Control (AAFCO) as it will ensure that the food is both safe and nutritious. You should look for brands of dog food that claim to have an 'AAFCO approved complete and balanced nutritional value' – it is illegal for a brand to claim that they have been approved by the AAFCO if they have not. Make sure the food you purchase contains protein, carbohydrates, fats, vitamins and minerals.

## How much to Feed Your Dalmatian

Unfortunately there is no exact method for figuring out exactly how much an individual Dalmatian should eat. Determining the correct size meal depends on the type of dog food, how many times a day your dog eats, your dog's size and weight, your dog's metabolic rate, the amount of exercise they get and many other possible variants. Adult Dalmatian are normally fed twice a day. I recommend looking at the feeding guide on the packaging of your dog's food. The feeding guide is normally recommends weights of food based upon your dog's weight. However this feeding guide is not necessarily accurate (your dog may struggle gaining weight or may gain weight at an increased rate). I recommend talking to your vet about how much you should be feeding your Dalmatian. It also takes a bit of time to get used to your Dalmatian and their eating habits.

## Visits to the Vet

It is important to take your Dalmatian to the vet on a regular basis. Regular visits to the vet can allow you to treat any issues your Dalmatian has in the early stages to avoid them having a negative impact on your

Dalmatian's health. I recommend scheduling to see your vet at least twice a year – however more frequent visits are advantageous in identifying health problems! It is more important to prevent the onset of disease rather than treat them once they occur. With each visit to the vet you should make sure that you get your dog weighed. By getting your dog weighed on a regular basis you will know if you are feeding it the correct sized portions.

## Exercise

Exercise is vitally important to keep your Dalmatian happy, healthy and behaving correctly. Dogs, and puppies, have a lot of energy and may develop destructive behaviors if they are not allowed to burn off their energy. How much exercise a dog needs is dependent on its age, breed and health. Most Dalmatian should be walked for at least 30 minutes a day – however I recommend walking your Dalmatian for around 60 minutes a day to ensure it has gotten enough exercise. You will know when your Dalmatian has had enough exercise when it has slowed its walking speed by a considerable amount. Good exercise uses both physical and mental muscles. I therefore recommend providing your Dalmatian with multiple different sources of exercise such as: hiking, walking around your block (using different routines), taking your Dalmatian to the park and taking your Dalmatian swimming. If you provide your Dalmatian with a lack of exercise they are likely to become obese. Obesity in Dalmatian, like in humans, comes with a wide range of health issues. Obesity contributes to a dog developing diabetes, respiratory disease, heart disease and general ill health and tiredness. I recommend living by the following philosophy: a tired dog is a happy, healthy and good dog.

# GROOMING

Grooming is an important aspect to caring for your Dalmatian! Grooming includes caring for your Dalmatian's coat, dental health, nails and over all cleanliness. Dogs enjoy getting messy so sometimes cleaning can be a chore! The following section will highlight all the aspects of grooming that you should consider.

## Grooming Tools

> **Bristle Brush:** Bristle brushes are used for all breeds of dog. Bristle brushes help to keep your dog's coat shiny and free from dirt.
> **Clippers and Shedding Blade:** Most species of dog will need to have their coats trimmed in summer to keep them cool. I recommend using clippers for dogs with long coats and shedding blades for short hair dogs.
> **De-Matting Rake:** De-matting rakes have long wire prongs. These prongs are great for removing matts from long coats. It is important to use this tool gently to avoid causing your dog discomfort.
> **Rubber Brush:** Rubber brushes are great for removing dead hair. They create a massaging

effect which many dogs enjoy.

➢ **Slicker Brush:** Slicker brushes are used to remove tangles and dead hair. They have rows of bent wire pins. They should only be used on dogs with long or thick hair.

➢ **Nail Clippers:** Nail clippers should be scissor shaped to allow for best control. It is important to purchase sharp nail clippers and to always have a spare set (in case one set become blunt).

➢ **Nail File:** Nail files are used to file the end of your dog's toe nail after it has been clipped. It is important to purchase a high quality nail file as it will allow the filing process to be completed much quicker.

## Grooming a Long Hair Dog

To groom a long haired Dalmatian you should first go over their coat with a slicker brush. Make sure that you are brushing your pet gently to avoid causing any discomfort to your Dalmatian as you remove tangles and dead hair. You should brush your dog's legs, tail, thighs, head and back. Once you have gone over the coat with a slicker brush you should then repeat the process with a bristle brush. Make sure to brush in the direction that the coat naturally settles in. The point of the bristle brush is to smooth out the detangled hair. Long haired dogs will need to be brushed on a daily basis. If you want to change the hairstyle of your Dalmatian I recommend using clippers. When using clippers it is first important to visualize how you want your Dalmatian's coat to look. You should use clippers on your dog's head, feet, legs, sides, underside and body. It is important to trim the fur away from your dog's eyes and muzzle – make sure to take extra care around your pet's eyes!

## Grooming a Short Haired Dog

Short haired Dalmatian should be brushed a minimum of once a week. Brushing your Dalmatian's coat will stimulate natural oils in their skin and will also remove any dead hair. You should groom your short haired Dalmatian by brushing all over its body with a slicker brush. Make sure to start at the head and work your way down. It is important to keep your Dalmatian's coat taut as you brush to effectively remove dead hair. Once you have removed all of the Dalmatian's dead hair you should brush the Dalmatian's coat back into the position it naturally lies in. I recommend using a bristle brush or a rubber brush for this process. You can also comb your dog's coat. A short haired dog will not have excessive tangles in its coat and a fine toothed brush is a perfect way to make your dog's coat look perfect!

## Bathing your Dog

Just like people, dogs need a good bathing schedule. Most Dalmatian only require a bath once a month. However if your dog enjoys rolling around in mud and getting especially dirty, you may have to bathe it more often. It is not recommended to bathe your Dalmatian more than once a week as it will lose the essential oils present on its skin. It is important to use a Dalmatian friendly shampoo and conditioner when bathing your Dalmatian as they are designed to not irritate your Dalmatian's skin. If your dog has especially sensitive skin it is possible to purchase medicated shampoo to decrease the chance of irritating your dog. I recommend washing your dog in either your bath tub or shower, as it is the least likely to create a watery mess! It is considered best practice to provide your pet with a non-slip mat to keep them secure in the shower or bath tub. Before bathing your dog make sure to have your shampoo and a towel ready to hand. While bathing your pet you should keep one hand on your Dalmatian at all times to make sure it does not leave the bath / shower. If your Dalmatian is worried about the bathing process reward them with treats to encourage them to relax. You should aim to massage your Dalmatian during the shampooing and toweling process to make the bathing experience more pleasurable and fun for them.

# Brushing your Dogs Teeth

In America it is estimated that 80% of dogs have some form of dental disease by 3 years of age! Dalmatian, like humans, need to have their teeth cleaned to remove bacteria and tartar build up. If you do not clean your Dalmatian's teeth they are likely to develop Periodontal disease which affects the base of the tooth near the gum line. Dalmatian can also suffer from dental disease such as gingivitis. It is recommend using a meat flavored toothpaste to reward your Dalmatian when it lets you brush its teeth – these toothpastes have the added benefit of being nontoxic if swallowed! You can use a regular toothbrush or a finger brush for the cleaning process. Make sure that the brush has soft bristle to avoid damaging your Dalmatian's teeth and gums. Aim to brush each individual tooth for around 5 seconds. It is considered best practice to brush your Dalmatian's teeth on a daily basis. Daily cleaning is the best way to prevent dental problems and to keep your Dalmatian's breath smelling dramatically better!

# Ear Cleaning

Dogs have very long ear canals (around 5 to 10cm in length) that have a right angled bend in them. The bend means that foreign objects can easily get into your Dalmatian's ear canal but are very hard to get out! If your Dalmatian gets water in its ear, the water can pool at the bend and cause ear infections due to the warm, moist and dark environment of the ear. You should ask your vet how often you should clean your Dalmatian's ears, but as a rule of thumb: no more than once a week and no less than once a month. To clean your Dalmatian's ears you will need ear cleaner, cotton wool and treats to reward your dog during the potentially uncomfortable process. There are multiple different brands of ear cleaner available and it is important to choose a good quality product. I recommend asking you vet for their suggestion as most pet stores will stock different brands. Once you have the products to hand it is time to start the cleaning process. Gently hold the flap of your dog's ear upright and fill the ear canal with the ear cleaner. It is important to aim the ear cleaner directly downwards as you use it. Once the ear cleaner is in place, massage the skin around your dog's ear to mix the ear cleaner with the contents of your Dalmatian's ear canal. Do this for around 20 seconds. Once the massaging time is up, stand up and move away from your dog. Your dog will shake its head vigorously to remove some of the ear cleaner. Once your dog has stopped shaking its head, grab the cotton wool and use it to wipe the folds at the opening of your Dalmatian's ear canal until it looks clean. Make sure to reward your Dalmatian before and after the ear cleaning process to relax it.

## Nail Clipping

It is important to trim your Dalmatian's toe nails every two weeks to keep them properly maintained. If you allow your pet's toe nails to grow too long it will cause your Dalmatian discomfort as it walks – the long term consequence of walking on overly long toe nails is arthritis! It is important to use clippers that resemble scissors as they provide the most control while clipping your Dalmatian's nails. It is also considered best practice to use small clippers as they again allow for better control. Make sure that your clippers are sharp before attempting to clip your pet's nails. Gently separate your Dalmatian's fingers for clipping – never squeeze your Dalmatian's toe as they will cause them to be in pain. It is considered best practice to have an assistant during the clipping process as they are able to secure your dog in place and distract it's attention. You should aim to make the clipping process and a positive experience so your dog feels at ease – use positive praise and treats to promote a positive atmosphere! It is IMPORTANT to note that all Dalmatian have a vein that run through their fingers called a 'quick.' If you cut off too much of your dog's nail it is possible to cut into the 'quick' which will cause your Dalmatian to bleed. Although not fatal it is still to be avoided as it will cause your pet unnecessary discomfort. If you do accidentally cut the 'quick' you should stop the bleeding by dabbing a little cornstarch onto the nail with a cotton swab. It is also possible to file your Dalmatian's nail or have a vet cut your pet's nails for you (although this will have a fee). If you are worried about trimming your dog's nails I recommend taking your Dalmatian to a vet once to have them demonstrate how to trim your pet's nails correctly.

# TRAINING

It would seem that Dalmatian enjoy being trained due to the fact that they both enjoy the human interaction of the training process and seem to enjoy 'pleasing' their owners. Training your Dalmatian is a perfect way to strengthen the bond between you and your pet as well as being a cool thing to show to non-dog owners.

## The Key Components of Training

The following bullet points are the five most important aspects of training any animal:

- Trust
- Positive reinforcement
- Repetition
- Patience
- Consistency

## Pre-requisites for successful training

It is vital that your Dalmatian are well socialized and accustomed to both your presence and being handled by you. It is not a good idea to try to train new Dalmatian immediately after purchasing them as they will not trust you and may be frightened or stressed by the training process. Younger Dalmatian, and puppies, are generally more adaptable to training and will therefore pick up new tricks at a faster rate. However younger Dalmatian will also have a shorter attention span which can make the process of training them a long process. Older Dalmatian will have a longer attention span but may be less willing to do physical based training.

## Preparation

Before starting to train your Dalmatian it is best to know how your Dalmatian enjoys spending it's time and what food it loves so you can reward it appropriately. It is important to find one or two healthy treats to reward your Dalmatian with to help them stay healthy and motivated during the training process. I recommend rewarding your Dalmatian with the following treats: raw carrot, a liver treat or a small piece of chicken. The reason it is important to know your pet Dalmatian's preferences is to allow you to work with your pet's natural inclinations and to praise and positively re-enforce the behavior you want.

## Clicker Training

Clicker training is considered the easiest and most effective way to train Dalmatian. The concept behind the training is that the clicker tells your Dalmatian when they have correctly performed a trick or action. Using a click also allows you to signal to your dog that they have done something correct from a long distance away. Clickers allow you to shape your dog's behavior, which means praising and rewarding closer and closer approximations to the behavior or trick you wish to teach. A click should always be paired with a treat. This allows your dog to create an association between 'clicks' and treats which will encourage your dog to obey clicks. You can purchase a specialized dog training clicker from any pet store or online. Before using the clicker in training, you should pair a click with a reward. Simply click then give your dog a treat. Then wait a few seconds and repeat the process. Repeat this around 10 to 15 times so your dog knows to associate clicks with treats before the training session has even begun.

## Teaching Focus and Attention

The fundamental aspect of training a Dalmatian is to teach the Dalmatian to pay attention to you. You should say the dog's name and then reward them for their attention once they give it to you. Repeat this process several times to ensure that your dog will respond with the appropriate level of attention when you call its name. It is important to shape your Dalmatian's behavior through positive reinforcement

until you can get your dog to give you full focus –
including eye contact.

## General Training Tips

The most important training tip is to make sure that
you always keep training session short. Short training
session will reduce the chance of your dog becoming
frustrated and will likewise enhance its concentration. I
recommend keeping all training session between 10 and
15 minutes in length. Remember to always reward your
Dalmatian after clicking to reinforce the likelihood that
they will obey clicks. If you are teaching a tricky
command, I recommend giving your dog a 'jackpot' of
treats when they do the desired trick. By giving your dog
more treats than normal will signify that they have done
the correct action. It is considered best practice to never
end on a failure! If your Dalmatian has not fully come to
terms with a new trick, you should end the training
session by rewarding your pet for completing a trick they
already know. This will keep your Dalmatian looking
forward to training sessions.

## Avoid Punishment

Dogs do not learn well by being punished.
Punishment will normally make your Dalmatian feel
confused, stressed and scared – which are not good

mental states to be in for learning! A dog that destroys a piece of furniture and looks guilty is responding to your anger rather than knowing what they did was wrong. If your dog is doing something destructive I recommend clapping your hands loudly, or calling its name, to get its attention. Once you have its attention you should lead its focus onto a more productive activity.

## What if the training is not working?

It is important that you go into the training process with the intention of having fun and bonding with your pet – any tricks your pet learns will be an added bonus! It is very uncommon for a Dalmatian to be untrainable. If the training is not working it is important to think about if you have a close relationship with the Dalmatian you are trying to train and if your Dalmatian is in the correct mind set to learn tricks. Dalmatian can easily become bored of repeated training and may likewise be disinterested due to the time of day. Another reason for a dog's disinterest may be that you are offering them the wrong type of treat as a reward. It is important to remember that dogs, like humans, learn at different rates and some Dalmatian will therefore take longer to train. If a Dalmatian seems impossible to train it is probably advisable to stop trying to train it and just enjoy playing with it and caring for it.

# TRAVELING WITH YOUR DOG FOR LOCAL TRIPS

Driving with a dog in your car can be problematic. Sometimes your dog will whine, bark, move around in a haphazard manner or even throw up. Driving can give some dogs anxiety which can lead to some unpleasant long drives! This section will outline 7 rules that will allow your pawed pet to feel more comfortable in the care – which will make both your, and your pets, traveling lives much more relaxing and enjoyable.

## Patience and Planning

The first most important thing to remember when introducing your dog to your car is that patience is definitely required. You should let your dog explore your car well in advance of their first car journey. If you introduce your dog to the car on the day of its first journey – this is probably too late and may lead to your dog suffering from anxiety or being over whelmed by the whole experience. It is important to plan a series of 'exercises' to introduce your dog to your car. Firstly, you could allow it to spend some time exploring your car: the back seats, the boots, the front seats and all the cubby holes. Secondly you could take your dog on a short practice car ride: maybe around your block or just forward and backwards on your drive. This is important as it lets your dog become comfortable with the motion of the car. Some dogs will become nervous at the unfamiliar motion but with reassurance, treats and patience they will be able become more comfortable with the car. Another useful technique is to feed your dog on the backseat of your car for a few days. This builds up a positive association with the car which can be invaluable for dogs with an especially nervous temperament.

## Mark the Territory with Scent

No matter how used to your car a dog will get, car rides will always be a source of excitement and adventure. This makes it highly important to allow your dog to mark their territory within your car. This could be done by allowing your dog to have a specific seat in the car, or boot, that they can identify as their space. This will allow them to become familiar with the space which will lead them to become more easily relaxed. One way to help your dog to mark its territory is to bring its favorite toys, blankets and cushions into the car. Adding your dog's favorite things, which will already be covered in their scent, is a great way to make your dog feel comfortable and relaxed in your car.

## Security

It is important to focus on the security and safety of your four-legged friend during all car excursions. This may mean that you install a partition between the passenger area and the boot of your car to stop your dog being able to disrupt your focus while driving. Other common methods to secure your dog are: dog carriers and specialized doggy seatbelts. It is important to note that different countries, states and areas may have completely different rules and regulations concerning transporting dogs in your car. It is important to look up the traffic codes in your local area and anywhere you wish to travel. This will ensure your dog is safe and may also avoid you receiving any unpleasant traffic violation fines.

## Pit Stops

While on a long drive everyone wants to have a break. For humans this might mean a snack and a coffee at a service station or a short break in a scenic area. When you are bringing your dog on the road with you, it is important to plan ahead. Check the route for pit stop destinations that will allow your dog to stretch their legs, go to the toilet, eat, drink and burn off some steam. Keeping a canine cooped up in a small space for a long period of time heightens the chance of your pet misbehaving or having a toilet accident. Most routes will have scenic walks, dog friendly establishments and rest areas that are suited for taking a quick break with your dog.

## Exiting the Vehicle

It is important to **ALWAYS** exit your vehicle before you let your dog exit. If you let your dog exit the car before you it could lead to traffic accidents, your dog running away or your dog running into the road. When exiting the vehicle, it is best practice to:

1. Check that your dog is secure
2. Ext the vehicle
3. Walk around to the exit closet to your dog (car door, window or trunk)
4. Make eye contact with your dog and give a clear command to stay
5. Open the exit
6. Give a command for your dog to exit
7. Attach a leash or harness if necessary

Giving clear commands to your dog allows for you to remain in control of the situation. This can also help nervous or excitable dogs to retain focus.

## Food and Water

It is important to limit your dog's food and water intake before a journey. If your pet has consumed to much food, they might throw up. If your pet has drank too much water, they may have to use the bathroom well in advance of your first pit stop. Both of these scenarios can lead to your dog feeling unwell, and it may also lead you to feeling unwell due to any unpleasant smells. It is important to limit the amount of snacking and drinking your dog can do in the car, but it is also important to provide sustenance for your dog during long trips. Finding the correct balance can take some time, as the balance is different for each dog. The best way to make sure a dog is unlikely to become travel sick during a journey is to allow them to build their confidence and comfortableness inside a moving vehicle on shorter practice journeys.

## Overheating

Dogs are prone to overheating while inside cars for prolonged periods of time. If you have to make a long journey with your dog, it might be a good idea to make a sheltered space. This could be done by laying a blanket over a section of your car or boot. A shadowy space can definitely help your dog keep cool. Another way to minimize discomfort for your dog on hot days is to provide them with cool water, ice cubes or a wet flannel you can put on their head. If you are planning on exiting your car and leaving your dog inside it is HIGHLY important to limit how long your dog is left inside the car. Dog can overheat very quickly and a car in direct sunlight can become unbearably hot for a dog. I suggest never leaving your dog in a locked car. Opening the car window slightly is not enough to keep your pet cool. Your dog's health and safety is of vital importance, don't take the chance and take your dog with you when you exit the car.

# TRAVELING WITH YOUR DOG INTERNATIONALLY

Most people purchase a dog when they have decided to settle down and start a family. Most people believe that it is difficult to travel internationally with a dog – this leads a lot of people to not want a dog during their young wanderlust years. What if I was to tell you that there are ways for a dog lover to travel internationally with their furry friend? Dogs are considered by many to be a human's best friend, why would you want to leave your best friend at home while you explore the world? Bring your dog with you!

## Where to travel with your dog

When you are planning your next adventure, it is important to consider the climate, time of year and weather forecast. For example, you would not want to take a long-haired dog to Africa during the heart of summer, similarly you would not want to take a breed like a Chihuahua to a cold climate during the winter months. Dogs generally are highly adaptive creatures, but it is not worthwhile acclimatizing your pet to dramatically different climates for the purpose of a short trip.

If you are planning on taking your dog to a very

different climate you can always take accessories to make the change in temperature easier to adapt to. For example, you can bring warm jumpers, coats and snow boots for you dog if you are going to a cold climate. If you are taking your dog to a hot climate you might consider bring it a pair of shoes (the hot ground can become uncomfortable for unprepared paws) or a cooling jacket. Cooling jacket can be filled with water and work similar to an ice pack. A cheap cooling jacket is the 'Go Fresh Pet Ice Colling Dog Vest' made by 'Pets at Home' and costs a reasonable $15.

When planning a trip with your pet it is important to take into account your pet's personality. Some dogs, like humans, do not like to be away from their homely comforts. If you are planning on traveling with your pet, it is advisable to take your dog with you everywhere during its puppyhood as a method of introducing it to the traveling lifestyle.

## Regulations

Before deciding on when and where to travel, it is first a good idea to check the regulations of the airlines, boarder control and transportation services you will encounter during your travel. Each country will have different regulations surrounding importing dogs. Some countries will have strict importation regulations surrounding pets, while others are more lenient.

If you are traveling from a rabies free country around mainland Europe most countries only require your pet to be microchipped and have had a rabies vaccination. However, countries such as the United Kingdom, Norway, Finland and Malta need your dog to have had an additional tapeworm treatment. If you are traveling from a country that is not rabies free you will need proof (proof last for a year) that your dog has had a rabies antibody blood test.

Some countries, such as Australia, have quarantine regulations which means your dog will have to be test on arrival by a government lab. This normally takes a minimum of ten days! For countries who have quarantine laws you will also need an important permit, veterinary certificates and recent rabies blood tests.

The most reliable source for checking the importation regulations is: www.pettravel.com. This website lists all the regulations for all the countries of the world and is an invaluable source for anyone looking to travel with their dog.

# Method of Travel

There are a lot of different methods to travel with your dog; by car, by plane, by boat, by coach and by train to name but a few. Each method of travel will raise its own problems and challenges.

If you are planning on taking your pet on a flight it is important to note that there are three main methods: taking your dog with you in the cabin of the plane, checking your dog as baggage or booking your dog to be taken on a separate cargo flight. Most airlines will have regulation that allow dogs of up to 46cm length, 28cm width and 24cm height with a maximum weight of 8kg. Most airlines will not allow you to have your dog outside of a container if it is traveling on the cabin. The reason for this is that airlines are worried dogs may run up and down the aisle during dinner time which may disturb other customers.

If a dog is too big for the cabin it will have to be checked as baggage. The baggage hold is temperature and pressure regulated so your pet will be fine once in the air. The only concern when checking your pet into the baggage hold is the fact that your pet will be exposed to the elements during loading and unloading. If you are leaving from, or arriving at, an especially cold airport this could cause your dog health problems.

Airports with high heat and humidity are also a concern – for example the Emirates airline will not allow dogs to be transported in baggage between 1st May and 30th September as the heat and humidity are dangerously high. When booking a flight with a pet please priorities short and direct flights if possible!

If you cannot fly with your pet, you can book your pet a flight with a cargo service. There are plenty of cargo services that specialize in the transportation of animals. The only downside of booking a cargo flight for your dog is that you and your dog may not arrive at the destination at the same time, or even day. Some cargo flights will also land at non-commercial airports – which can mean you have to travel to pick up your pet once at your destination.

Most commercial boat lines have kennels on board. Most boat lines have a regulation that once onboard all dogs must stay in their kennels. This is to prevent the potential for accidental an overboard. It is important to note that on long journeys this may not be the best option as boat line kennels are not always the most comfortable and spacious.

Most trainlines worldwide will allow dogs to be transported upon them. Some trainline companies have regulation that dogs have to be on a leash or in a dog crate for the entirety of the journey. Some countries, such as Vietnam, do not allow dogs on trains,

Traveling by car is by far the best option! It allows you to control the pace of your journey and to allow your four-legged friend to have as many pit stops, food breaks and exercise breaks. Car journeys are also least likely to cause your dog stress as they are likely to be a normal occurrence.

## Traveling Equipment

Here is a useful list of equipment you can purchase to make traveling with your dog easier:

- A waist harness: A waist harness will allow you to keep your hands free while keeping your dog in control and next to you. Waist harnesses are especially useful for anyone hiking as it allows you to fully access your map. Waist harnesses are also very useful when you need two hands to transport your luggage to the correct location.
- IATA (International Air Transportation Association) pet crate: An IATA pet crate will help minimize any problem you may have checking your dog into the baggage compartment of a plane or keeping it in the cabin with you. Most airlines will accept crates with air holes on all sides, made of a sturdy plastic, have a wire door and have a secure locking

system. It is best practice to purchase a IATA crate though as it will definitely lead to less potential hassle.

- Pet Passport: Some countries, including all countries within Europe, require your pet to have their own passport. Pet passports state when you pet has last received vaccination for diseases – such as rabies. Most vets will issue pet passports but if they do not, I would recommend asking the vet to tell you where the closest location to get a pet passport is. Pet passports come with a lot of space for you to update the medical history of your pet.

## Arrival

Having a fixed plan for your arrival can definitely help to minimize stress, for yourself and your dog. Have you booked accommodation that allows for pets? Have you plotted a route that will allow you easy access to food and water for your dog? Have you checked, and abided by, all local laws concerning dogs? As previously mentioned, flying your pet on a pet specific cargo flight is a highly popular choice. If this is the case – have you planned to get to where the cargo flight is landing? Have you made accommodations for your dog to be looked after if you cannot get to them straight away? Please don't ruin your trip through lack of preparation!

# BREEDING

We previously did not include a section on how to breed dogs. The main reason for this is that this series of books is designed for first time dog owners and beginners. Breeding is a complicated and potentially risky business. One of the main reasons I decided to not include a breeding section is that breeding laws are widely different from country to country. Before beginning to breed any animal, you should check the local laws, regulations and best practices. However due to popular demand the following section will give a **BREIF** overview on the breeding process. This guide should not be used as your only resource if you plan to become a breeder!

**IMPORTANT NOTE:** IF YOU ARE SERIOUS ABOUT BECOMING A DOG BREEDER, I **URGE** YOU TO CONTACT YOUR LOCAL KEENLE CLUB AND ASK FOR ADVICE, OR SOMEONE THEY CAN PUT YOU IN TOUCH WITH. BREEDING DOGS CAN LEAD TO A PLETHORA OF PROBLEMS. HEIR ON THE SIDE OF SAFTEY AND PLEASE ASK YOUR LOCAL KENNEL CLUB FOR HANDS ON ADVICE AND SUPPORT.

# Before Breeding Begins

Dog breeding has been a big part of human history – dogs have been donned 'man's best friend' for a reason. Before breeding a litter, it is important to first gain as much information as you can. You should spend time studying the 'breed standard,' which will give you an outline on what a 'perfect' specimen of that breed will look and behave like. The AKC is has an amazing set of resources about breeding such as: illustrated guides, video guides and many written guides. Before breeding you must prepare yourself for the trails, successes, unexpected surprises and potential heart breaks that come hand in hand with the breeding process.

Before breeding it is important to assess the quality of your dog. Every loving dog owner thinks that their dog is the best, most loveable and cutest dog in the world. This idea does not always help in the breeding process. If you plan on breeding your current dogs it would be a good idea to assess their 'quality' before breeding them. This can be done by entering your dog into a dog show, this will allow you to compare your dog to other dogs in their breed. It is important to remember that breeding is about 'improving' the quality, temperament and physical health of your litter.

Before breeding it is important to note that raising

a litter of puppies is a hard and long full-time job! While it is very easy to romanticize the idea of caring for a group of puppies, the reality can be very tiring, time consuming, messy and at time over whelming. Some puppies can become semi uncontrollable during the weaning phase. The extra feeding, grooming, training, trips to the vet and vet bills can add up in time and money. Another important aspect to breeding is making sure that your puppies go to good homes. This can mean researching, background checking and screening potential owners. Breeding is a big commitment!

## Choosing a mating pair

The first thing to consider when you are starting the breeding process is; do you want to breed purebred dogs or mixed dogs? If want to make mixed dogs the coupling process can be easier. If you want to make purebred dogs it is important to choose a Dam (bitch) and a Sire (male dog) that have been registered to a Kennel Club. If both the Sire and Dam are registered to a Kennel Club the litter can be automatically registered.

When you are selecting a breeding partner for your dog the most important thing to remember is to pick a coupling that compliments each other. Choose a partner that comes from a strong blood lines, have no health problems, has a good temperament and matches the type of coat you want your litter to have. For example, if your dog has a 'bad' coat it may be worth coupling them with a dog that comes from a long line of dogs with 'good' coats. While this idea may seem simple in principle it can actually be very difficult – when looking at a dog it is very difficult to actually comprehend their strengths and weaknesses in a cohesive way. It is best practice to write down the strengths of a dog and then write down its weaknesses. This gives you a resource to go home and think over your choice. When it comes to breeding being particular is not a bad thing!

The most important factors to considers are health and temperament.

Health issues are hereditary in dogs. You should ask the owner of any potential mates to provide a medical history for their dog and their dog's ancestor (if possible). As a breeder one of your main goals should be to breed dogs that do not suffer from any of the main illnesses, genetic deformities and diseases that affect dogs (there will be an outline of the most common diseases, illnesses and genetic problems that affect dogs in a later section). Temperament is mostly a hereditary trait. This can allow you track the temperaments of your dog and your dog's potential mates. It is not worth breeding your dog with a 'perfect' breed standard dog if it has a nasty, misbehaving or mean temperament.

If you do not own the dog you are choosing as your dog's mating partner, you will have to create and finalize a stud contract. A stud contract should include fees, obligations and who has ownership of the litter of puppies. Stud contracts may include payment of cash, a 'pick of the litter' or a designated number of puppies from the litter (this can be done as a lottery or by the choice of the litter's owner). A stud contract should be signed by both parties and both parties should receive a copy of the finalized contract.

## Importance of Genetics

As previously mentioned, – your dog's health and temperament will be determined by the genetics passed down to them by their parents and grandparents. It is important to note that, like in humans, hereditary problems are capable of skipping on or two generations. Do not judge the 'quality' of a dog based on its temperament and aesthetic alone. Genetics are not obvious by looking at a dog, interacting with a dog or listening to a dog – this is why it is important to examine the pedigree of your potential mating couple. It is important to become knowledgeable about the genetic problems that tend to affect your breed. The following is a quick guide on how to spot potential problems:

- Dominant Genetics – some diseases, illnesses and genetic disorders follow a dominant genetic pattern. A dominant genetic is one that will always be passed on and only need one mutant gene. If only one of the parents carried a dominant gene, then the disorder will appear in all subsequent generations.
- Recessive Genes – some disorders can only appear in dogs that have one mutant gene from their mother and one mutant gene from their father. Dogs who suffer from these genetics are called homozygous. Dogs who only have one mutant gene are called heterozygous. Both homozygous and heterozygous dogs will pass their mutant genetics on to their offspring. Recessive mutant gene can pass through generations dormant until a mating couple, who both carry the gene, are paired together. It is **VERY** important to research the medical history of your breeding couple's ancestry.
- Polygenic Disorders – Polygenic disorders are a result of the action of multiple 'bad' genes. Polygenic disorders are very difficult to track as it is hard to determine what concoction of genes is creating the disorder. Polygenic disorders can sometimes appear as either a Dominant gene or a Recessive gene which makes them especially hard to identify.

## Pre-Breeding Health Checks

The vital steps in producing a good 'quality' litter of puppies happens well in advance of the actually mating process. It is important to ensure that the mating pair have had recent medical checks. Mating pairs need to have had multiple screenings for genetic problems, have had regular visits to the vets, have had a nutritious diet and received enough exercise. Bitches should not be overweight before the mating begins. It is a good idea to thoroughly exercise both dogs until they are toned and well-muscled. It is important to note that a Bitch who is in a good mental state will produce a better litter and will also provide better care to their young.

It is a good idea to have both of the mating pair test for brucellosis. Brucellosis is an infectious form of bacteria that can lead to sterility and spontaneous abortions. Both of the breeding pair should also be completely up to date on their vaccinations and good through a pre-breeding physical performed by a vet.

The age in which your dog becomes sexually active is dependent on the purity of the breed, the dog's ancestral history and their genetics. Male dogs will normally become fertile at around 6 months of age, hit their full sexual maturity at around 12-15 months and are capable of breeding well into their old age. Female dogs normally go into 'heat' (also known as Estrus) at around 6 months – although it can occur later. Female dogs will enter heat at intervals of approximately 6 months until their old age. It is important to note that most Kennel Clubs will not allow a litter to be registered if their mother is under 8 months of age. It is considered best practice to not breed a bitch during her first heat. This is due to the fact that most breeders believe it to be uncompassionate to put a young animal through the physical and mental stress associated with lactation, pregnancy and giving birth. It is also considered best practice to not breed a female dog on consecutive heats as their bodies need time to recuperate after pregnancy.

## How To Identify If Your Female Dog Is Fertile

The following section will give a guideline on how to know whether or not your bitch is ready for breeding. There are four main stages in a female dog's cycle: Proestrus, Estrus, Diestrus, Anestrus.

- Proestrus: – Proestrus is the phase that begins before a female goes into heat. Proestrus can be identified by bloody vaginal discharges and your dog having a swollen vulva. This phase last for around 9 days and will involve your female dog attract potential mates. No breeding will take place during this period.

- Estrus: - Estrus lasts for around 9 days. This is when the mating process will take place. The female will accept being fertilized by the male during this period. Ovulation normally occurs during the first 48 hours of Estrus. Some females will allow multiple mating session – others will not. It is considered best practice to try and initiate a mating session between the 48-hour and 72-hour mark.

- Diestrus: - Diestrus lasts for around 2 to 3 months. During this period the female's reproductive tract is under the control of their progesterone hormone. This will happen whether or not the female dog has become pregnant.

- Anestrus: - During Anestrus the female dog will have no interest in sexual contact. This period lasts for between 3 and 4 months.

## Natural Breeding

When it comes to natural breeding, most breeders will introduce the mating pair around the 10th or 13th day after the onset of proestrus. If the mating process is successful, most breeders will encourage the pair to mate every other day for two to three attempts.

It is important to note that proestrus is not visible in a lot of female dogs. It is considered best practice to have a vet examine your dog's hormones in advance of the mating process.

Female dogs are generally less inhibited by their environment during the mating process. This makes it a common practice for the female dog to be taken to the male dog for the breeding. Male dogs are much more territorial and therefore feel more comfortable mating in environments they feel confident in. Breeding involving young studs and experienced bitches tend to go most smoothly. It is not uncommon for a handler to assist in guiding young dogs during the process. It is a good idea to determine who will assist in the breeding during the finalization of the stud contract.

During the mating process, the male will mount the female from the rear. Penetration and ejaculation can be incredibly quick or a slow process – it depends on the confidence, experience and compatibility of the mating pair. After ejaculation occurs the stud and bitch will not separate for around 15 to 30 minutes. This is known as a 'tie.' It is **HIGHLY** important to not attempt to separate the mating pair during a 'tie.' A 'tie' occurs because the stud's penial gland engorges effectively 'trapping' the pair together. This is a biological method employed across the animal kingdom and is implemented to heighten the chance of a successful fertilization. Attempting to separate the mating pair during a 'tie' can lead to the mating failing or the genitals of both dogs being injured. After the pair is ready – they will separate naturally.

## Artificial Insemination

Artificial Insemination is implemented when natural breeding is impractical. Most Kennel Clubs will accept and register litters who have been created through artificial insemination. However, they will only accept litters produced with fresh sperm, extended sperm or frozen sperm. Artificial insemination is a simple process. It involves transferring the sperm into the female's vagina, near the cervix. If you are considering using artificial insemination, please seek the assistance of your vet as they are trained, and qualified, in the procedure.

## Nutrition for a Pregnant Dog

A healthy bitch should continue her diet. Her pregnant caloric intake should match what her regular caloric intake is. **HOWEVER**, as her body weight increases so must her caloric intake – this occurs around 5 weeks before whelping. You should gradually increase your dog's caloric intake until it is about 135-150% of what it normally is. Some dogs will not want one or two large meals – it is therefore considered best practice to start offering your dog smaller, but more frequent, meals.

# Whelping and the Whelping Box

Whelping is the term given to the act of a female dog giving birth. Most whelping happens inside the whelping box – a designated area for the birthing to happen. It is important to create the whelping box well in advance of your dog's due date. This will give her time to become accustomed and used to the whelping area, which helps to minimize stress during the birthing. If a whelping boxing is accepted and known, your dog might choose her own whelping area. This could be your closet, behind the couch or in the bath – which can lead to a lot of mess and a lot of discomfort.

A perfect whelping box would have the following traits: dry, warm, quiet, draft-free and secluded. A good whelping box will also have low sides to allow ease of access during the pregnancy. It is considered best practice to have a small shelf on the side of the whelping box. This shelf will allow puppies to move out of the way of their still birthing mother. This allows the puppies to stay safe and also not distract their mother. A shelf is less necessary if you are watching the birthing and are actively moving the puppies to a nearby safe location. Most breeders line the whelping box with newspaper as it can easily be changed when soiled. After the whelping, the flooring is normally changed to a clean towel or a bath mat.

# A List Of Suggest Whelping Equipment

Below is a list of all the supplies you will need during a whelping. This list is not the be all and end all of whelping equipment. Don't be afraid to make some alterations or additions to this list.

- Newspaper: - Newspaper can be used as an initial bedding for the mother and puppies. This can be used to line before, during and after the whelping.
- Bath Mats: - Bath mats can be used after the whelping is completed to give the puppies a better surface to stand on. If you are going to use a bath mat, make sure it is a non-slip bath mat to avoid unnecessary falls.
- Clean Towels: - Clean towels can be used to line the whelping box before, during and after the whelping. Clean towels can also be used to clean puppies after they have been birthed.

- Thermostat: - A thermostat can be used to check the temperature of your dog before she beings the whelping. A overly high or low temperature can be a signal of complications.

- Dental Floss: - Dental floss can be used to sever the puppy's umbilical cords. If you are using dental floss please make sure it isn't waxed, scented or flavored.

- Shelf: - As previously mentioned a shelf in the whelping box can help to protect puppies after birth.

- Heating Pad: - A Heating pad can be extremely useful for keeping puppies warm after the birthing.

- Scissors: - Scissors can be used to cut the puppy's umbilical cord and placenta. Make sure to use stainless steel scissors to minimize the chance of infection. Please use a new pair of scissors or a pair that has been sterilized (in boiling water).

- Iodine: - Iodine is useful to clean the puppy's abdominal region after their umbilical cord has been cut.

# Signs Labor Is Approaching

The first sign that labor is approaching is that your dog will start building a an area to give birth. Hopefully this area is the designated whelping box. If your dog starts preparing an area that is not the whelping box you can try to encourage them to shift their 'nest' using treats and praise. If not you might have to make accommodation for your dog's chosen location.

Around 24 hours before the whelping commences, your dog's temperature will drop by 2-4 degrees. After the temperature drops, your dog's cervix will begin to dilate and the birth canal will open. During this period your dog may appear stressed, start panting and move around restlessly. This is perfectly normal and is nothing to worry about. Soon after this your dog will start straining and will start to give birth.

It is **VERY** important to keep your vet's number and the number of the local emergency clinic at hand during this process. Please contact your vet or the emergency clinic if any of the following things happen:

- Your dog is indicating they are in extreme pain
- Strong contractions are occurring, but birthing is not happening

- More than 2 hours passes between the birthing of puppies
- Your dog passes our or collapses
- Your dog passes a bloody or dark green fluid before the birth of the first puppy. (It is important to note that this is nothing to concern yourself with if the blood/green fluid is expelled after/during the birth of the first puppy)
- No signs of contractions, labor or preparation for labor occurs after 64 days of your dog's last mating session.
- One or more of the puppies are still born.

## Aftercare

It is not uncommon for a female dog to not want to eat or drink much for 1 or 2 days after whelping. After this 2 day 'fast' they will need a high amount of nutrients and calories. If you have been feeding your dog a healthy diet and proper food, they will not need supplementation. If your dog goes for a long period without having proper nutrition, they may develop eclampsia. Eclampsia can be spotted by a dog whimpering excessively, a dog staggering or spasming, nervousness and unsteadiness. Eclampsia is an easily treatable condition but can be fatal if untreated. After whelping your female dog should return to the weight she was before breeding. For two or three weeks you will need to double or triple your dog's food intake. It is considered best practice to split your dog's feeding into 3 or 4 meals a day to avoid stress on their abdominal region.

There is a possibility that your bitch will suffer from a condition known as 'Canine Mastitis.' This condition will make her breasts a combination of firm to the touch (almost hard), red, hot, swollen and/or painful. If you think your bitch is suffering from this condition, contact a vet immediately! Canine Mastitis can happen for a few reasons: scratches from a puppy's claws or teeth, an infection or the puppies being weaned too early. A dog suffering from this condition may stop eating, stop allowing her puppies to feed or may generally just become agitated. While this condition is not necessarily fatal it can severely affect the calorie intake of the mother and puppies – which in turn can become fatal.

## Caring For New Born Puppies

Puppies are relatively easy to look after. They require warmth, such as a heating pad, until they are able to thermoregulate their body temperature. If your puppies are overly cold, it can lead to stress and an increased chance of infection and illness. If your puppies are overly hot, it can lead to death. When setting up a pen for your puppies it is considered best practice to have a heating pad on one side of the pen and a cooler space on the other side. This will allow puppies to easily regulate their temperature. Puppies need an atmospheric temperature of around 90 degrees for the first 5 days of their lives. After the first week, this temperature can be steadily lowered until it reaches a temperature of 75 degrees at the end of the fourth week of life.

After whelping your bitch will be producing highly nutritious and high calorie milk. This milk is known as 'colostrum.' Your new puppies will need to consume colostrum as quickly as possible, at least within the first 24 hours of their life. Colostrum contains immunoglobulins which help to protect the new born puppies from infections that the mother is immune to.

Some puppies will be ignored, or 'orphaned,' by their mother and will have a hard time feeding. These puppies may have to be fed by hand. It is important to remember that cow's milk, a non-dairy substitute or any other milk is not going to contain the nutrients, immunoglobulins and calories of a mother's colostrum milk. You may have to double the amount an 'orphaned' puppy consumes to make up for the lack of calories and nutrients. It is important to note that puppies grow and gain weight very quickly. You will have to adjust the amount you hand feed a puppy each day. You should gradually increase the puppy's intake as they will be receiving twice as much fluid as their peers. Before feeding you should warm the formula to boy temperature to simulate the mother's breast.

**Note:** Never produce more milk than is necessary and do not store it for more than one use. Milk is a great medium for bacteria growth! You do not want to feed your puppy something that could lead them to get ill.

## Weaning

There are many different ideas and schools of thought concerning when and how to wean puppies. You should discuss a weaning regiment with your vet to make sure that they understand how the dogs are feeding – this can help the vet deal with any complications if they arise. Most puppies will start the weaning process at around 2 to 5 weeks of age. Some breeders create 'gruel' for their puppies. This 'gruel' is a mixture of milk formula, ground dog food and water. Other breeders will offer their puppies a bowl full of warm milk. Weaning can take experimentation and experience. I highly suggest consulting your local Kennel Club, local breeders and your vet for advice.

To avoid an upset stomach, you should introduce the new feeding regiment slowly. Make sure to monitor your puppies for the first few weeks of the weaning process to make sure they are not throwing the food up!

# ILLNESSESS

There are multiple factors that play a huge part on your Dalmatian's health: your dog's genetics, the quality of veterinary care they receive, what they eat and how safe the environment they live in is. The following section aims to help you recognize the most common and major threats to your dog's health to allow you to treat and prevent them. Your Dalmatian's health is vitally important to giving your Dalmatian a chance at a long, happy and healthy life.

## Hip Dysplasia

Hip dysplasia is a heritable condition that prevents the thighbone from fitting snugly into the hip joint. Hip dysplasia is common among Dalmatian but does not affect them all. It normally has symptoms of pain and lameness. However, hip dysplasia does not always cause your Dalmatian discomfort but it may develop into arthritis as your Dalmatian ages. Hip dysplasia is incurable and Dalmatian who have it should not be bred. When purchasing a puppy from a breeder you should ask for proof that neither of your puppy's parents have hip dysplasia.

## Parasites

Dogs enjoy spending a lot of time outside where they lick and sniff everything, roll around in dirt and puddles and run through long grass. While they find these activities enjoyable they also lead to parasite infestations.

> ➢ **Fleas and Ticks:** Fleas and ticks are the most common parasites. Fleas breed incredibly quickly and a couple can turn into an infestation surprisingly quickly. Ticks can cause some very dangerous disease – such as Lyme Disease and Ehrlichoisis. You dog will repeatedly itch itself, either with its paw or against furniture, if it has a tick or flea infestation.
>
> ➢ **Skin Mites:** Skin mites are dramatically smaller than fleas and ticks. Skin mites live on, or burrow into, your Dalmatian's skin and can cause sever discomfort and diseases such as Mange. The main symptoms of skin mites are itching, skin irritation, inflammation and hair loss.
>
> ➢ **Heartworms:** Heartworms are parasites that migrate through your Dalmatian's internal system to their hearts and other major organs. Due to the locations they infest, they

are extremely dangerous and usually deadly! The most effective way to prevent heartworms is to use a monthly heartworm preventive – medication that can purchased from your vet. There are no symptoms for heartworms other than your Dalmatian becoming very ill.

- **Intestinal Worms:** Intestinal worms are very common among puppies. If your dog has recently had a tick or fleas there is a good chance that they now have an intestinal tapeworm. If your Dalmatian eats other Dalmatian's feces there is also a high chance that they will have an intestinal worm of some sort. The most common way to know if your Dalmatian has worms is to physically see the worms in your Dalmatian's waste. The best method to keep your Dalmatian worm-free is to have a vet perform a fecal test at least once a year.
- **Single Cell Parasites:** Single cell parasites live in your dog's digestive tract. They can cause both Giardia and Coccidiosis if left untreated. If you are giving your dog heartworm preventative medication you normally do not need to worry about single cell parasites as the medication should kill them as well.

## Cherry Eye

Cherry eye is a problem that more commonly affects certain breeds but can affect any dog. The main symptom of cherry eye is a large red swelling appearing at the inner corner of one your dog's eye. Cherry eye is caused by the prolapsing of a tear gland attached to your dog's third eyelid. The prolapsed gland swells forward and creates the red bulge. Cherry eye is not a vision threating illness but does cause your Dalmatian a lot of discomfort. There are a lot of websites and guides for curing cherry eye at home but I recommend taking your Dalmatian to the vet so it receives the best quality medical care from a trained professional. There are two surgical options, performed under general anesthetic, to treat cherry eye. The first is to remove the damaged tear gland completely. The second it to surgically manipulate the gland back into its correct position. I advise that you consult with your vet as to what the best course of action is for your Dalmatian's specific case.

## Incontinence

Incontinence can affect your Dalmatian at any age. If your Dalmatian has previously been housetrained, it is important to remember that a loss of bladder, or bowel, control is a physical problem not a behavioral one. Incontinence is most commonly found in older

Dalmatian, especially females. Incontinence is normally caused by the following reasons: a urinary tract infection, old age, stress and anxiety, neurological problems (such as seizures), recent spaying surgery, diseases and other health problems. If your dog is suffering from incontinence it is recommend to bring it straight to the vet. The vet will be able to diagnose what is causing the problems and will be able to provide a suitable solution.

## Parvovirus

Canine parvovirus is the both highly contagious and most deadly viral disease that affects dogs and puppies. Puppies have an increased chance of catching this illness. Most un-vaccinated dogs who catch parvovirus will die. However, parvovirus is not a fatal illness is identified in its early stages. The best method to prevent parvovirus is to give your puppy, and Dalmatian, a full course of medical shots to provide it with strong protection and immunity from the virus. It is also vital to keep your puppy away from other Dalmatian and animals before they have been fully vaccinated! The symptoms for parvovirus are: vomiting, lethargy, a fever and diarrhea. These symptoms are very common for a lot of other less serious illnesses but you should still take your pet to the vet if you notice any as you do not want to risk your dog having untreated parvovirus.

## Dental Problems

Most dental problems in dogs are cause by periodontal disease. Periodontal disease can affect more than just your Dalmatian's mouth and gums! If your Dalmatian has rotten teeth and highly damaged gums they are more likely to catch other illnesses. More dental hygiene can cause your Dalmatian to commonly get inflammations throughout their body. The best way to provide your dog with top quality dental care is to provide it with a chew toy. Chew toys allow your dog to strengthen their teeth and jaw as well as removing tartar! There are also multiple different types of doggy dental treats available which are designed to clean your dog's teeth and freshen their breath – Win Win! It is also considered best practice to clean your Dalmatian's teeth, either by taking your pet to a professional dental cleaning service, a veterinary clinic or by brush your Dalmatian's teeth yourself using a toothbrush. You should strive to make dental care a core part of your dog's grooming routine. The key signs for a dental disease are: excessive drooling, loss of appetite, difficulty eating, broken teeth, loose teeth, inflamed gums, tartar buildup and very pale gums. If you notice any of the above symptoms I recommend taking your dog to the vets.

## Ear Problems

The majority of ear problems are relatively easy to treat once they are diagnosed. Ear problems can either be chronic (reoccurring) or acute (one off). Ear infections are one of the most common type of ear problem found in Dalmatian. Ear infections normally occur in the external ear canal and have symptoms of ear redness, scabs and discharge around your dog's ear canal. This type of ear infection is called 'Otitis' and is caused by either a bacterial infection, a yeast or fungal infection, allergies or over exposure to water (such as swimming and bathing). The second most common type of ear problem is an infestation of ear mites. If your dog has ear mites there will be symptoms of black discharge around the ear canal, redness and inflammation of the ear canal, scabbing and a very strong odor. It is best practice to take your dog to the vet if they have any of the above symptoms as the vet will be able to identify the cause of the problem and be able to provide your dog with the best type of medical care. It is considered best practice to not clean your dog's ears before taking them to the vet – your vet will need to see the symptoms of your dog's ear problem. Most ear problems can be corrected through a treatment of oral medication or ear drops.

# DANGEROUS FOODS

When owning any pet it is important to know what you should and should not be feeding it. Dogs are no exception to this! There are multiple different foods that can cause sever health problems in Dalmatian – some can even be fatal! Foods that are commonly eaten by humans (both healthy foods and indulgent foods) can be incredibly toxic to Dalmatian. It is important to educate your family and guests on what a Dalmatian can and can't eat to avoid someone feeding it something that could damage its health. The following section will outline foods that you should NEVER give to your dog:

## Avocado

Avocado leaves, pits, bark and fruit contain a toxin called 'Persin.' While Persin is harmless to humans it has been known to cause breathing difficulties, stomach problems and fluid retention and buildup in the chest. An Avocado's pit is also incredibly dangerous as it will obstruct your Dalmatian's gastrointestinal tract if swallowed.

## Grapes and Raisins

Both grapes and raisins have been known to cause seriously health problems in Dalmatian – such as liver damage and kidney failure! It is not currently known what specific chemical in grapes and raisins is toxic to Dalmatian. It takes as little as a handful of grapes to seriously poison your dog!

## Chocolate

While chocolate is viewed as a treat for humans, it is definitely not for dogs. Chocolate contains a chemical called theobromine which is toxic to Dalmatian. Theobromine will cause a dog to vomit and have diarrhea. It also has the potential to cause seizures and long term damage to your pets nervous system and heart! It is important to watch children around your dog as they may, with the best intentions, feed your Dalmatian some of their chocolate.

## Coffee and Caffeine

Both coffee and caffeinated products can be fatal if ingested in a high enough quantity. Coffee and caffeine have similar negative effects to chocolate. It causes vomiting, abnormal heart palpitations, seizures and long term damage to the dog's nervous system. It is important to remember that caffeine can be found in a high number of products such as: energy drinks, tea, chocolate, cocoa beans and medicine.

## Macadamia Nuts

It can take as little as five macadamia nuts to have a seriously negative effect on your dog's health. The symptoms of macadamia nut poisoning include muscle tremors, vomiting, rapid breathing, rapid heartrate, increase body temperature and signs of general weakness. If macadamia nuts are mixed with chocolate the combination of poisoning will nearly always be fatal.

## Xylitol

Xylitol is a sugar based alcohol that can commonly be found in gum, candy, sweet baked goods and other sugar-substitute items. Xylitol causes no apparent harm to humans but is extremely toxic to dogs. Even a small dose of Xylitol can cause seizures, low blood sugar levels, liver failure and even death in Dalmatian!

## Yeast

Yeast can be found in basically any dough products (bread, cakes, etc). Yeast will rise and expand in your Dalmatian's stomach in a similar manner to how it rises in bread. A small amount of yeast will cause your dog mild discomfort and to be gassy. However if your dog ingests too much yeast it is likely rupture their stomach lining and intestines! It is important to never feed your dog bread or any other products containing yeast.

## Onions, Garlic and Chives

It does not matter what form these produces are in (powdered, raw, cooker, dehydrated or mixed with other foods) they are always detrimental to your Dalmatian's health. Onions, garlic and chives contain sulfoxides and disulfides which can cause anemia and damage to your Dalmatian's red blood cells. Onions, garlic and chives also cause vomiting, breathlessness and general weakness in Dalmatian.

## Peaches, Pears and Plums

Peaches contain pits that are potentially a choking hazard to dogs. The pits also contain amygdalin which contains a compound made up of cyanide and sugar that degrades into hydrogen cyanide when metabolized. Hydrogen cyanide is incredibly toxic to dogs and will normally lead to death! Pear seeds contain a small amount of arsenic which is likewise dangerous. Plum pits cannot be digested properly and will therefore cause intestinal obstruction which can cause multiple dangerous health issues. It is important to check your backyard for any trees that produce large fruits and seeds. If you find multiple seeds in your dog's waste it is probably best to cut down and remove the tree.

## Cooked Bones

There is a common misconception that all bones are good for Dalmatian. While chewing uncooked bones can help improve the strength of your Dalmatian's jaw and provide them with need nutrients, cooked bones are highly dangerous. Cooked bones can easily splinter into sharp, and jagged, pieces. These sharp splinters can tear the lining of your dog's throat or stomach. They will also cause your dog a lot of discomfort as they pass the splintered pieces of bone.

## Alcohol

Alcohol has the same effect on a dog's liver and brain as it has on a humans. However the effects of alcohol are greatly amplified on dogs and it therefore takes a lot less alcohol to cause damages – the smaller the dog the greater the effects. A small amount of alcohol can cause vomiting, diarrhea, depression, difficulty breathing, comas and death! Alcohol can obviously be found in beer, liquor and wine but can also been found in some food.

## Other Substances to Avoid

The following substances are considered less harmful but should still not be given to your Dalmatian:

chewing gum, baby food, apple seeds, corn on the cob, fat trimmings, salmon, tuna, milk and dairy, tobacco, salt, raw meat and raw eggs.

# EXTRA THINGS TO CONSIDER

The following sections are extra things to consider that did not fit into any of the above sections.

## Vacation

It is likely that you will have a vacation at some point during your Dalmatian's life. It is important to remember that not all vacations will accommodate your pet Dalmatian. It is therefore best practice to try and line up at least 3 people who would be willing to care for your pet Dalmatian while you are away, before even purchasing a Dalmatian. Some pet care stores provide a care service for owners while they are on holiday so it is also advisable to ask your local pet store if they offer this service. Another alternative is kennels and boarding services.

## Pack Animals

Dogs are pack animals and enjoy being social with humans, other animals and other Dalmatian. If you are going to be away from home for long periods of time (for example at work) it is considered best practice to purchase more than one Dalmatian. It is important that your Dalmatian does not feel lonely as this will lead to depression and unnecessary stress.

# Begging

If your Dalmatian begs for food at the table, you are not alone! Begging can seem cute at first but can quickly become an annoying habit. If begging goes unchecked it can escalate into whining during meal times, jumping up onto the table and ever stealing food off plates. The best way to avoid begging is to NEVER allow anyone to feed your Dalmatian from the table in the first place.
However if you have already fed your dog from the table I recommend ignoring your dog's begging. Once your pet realizes that begging is a futile process they will quickly stop it. Rewarding your dog when it is away from the table, during mealtimes, is the best way to encourage it to stop begging.

# Introducing a New Baby to your Dog

Dogs can become jealous. Jealousy can happen in any breed. All breeds, from Rottweilers to Pugs, have been known to bite or attack babies out of pure jealousy. The best way to make sure that your Dalmatian does not become jealous is to keep to your established care routine. Do not forget to feed, walk, bathe, train and play with your Dalmatian! The first way to introduce your new baby to your Dalmatian is to introduce its scent. Bring your Dalmatian an item that has your baby's scent on it (such as an item of clothing) and allow your dog to become familiar with the scent. You need to make it clear that your dog needs your permission to sniff the item – this will create clear boundaries and create respect for the baby. Before introducing your Dalmatian to the baby it is considered best practice to take your Dalmatian for a long walk to drain it of any excess energy. It is important to make sure that the baby, the Dalmatian and yourself remain calm during the introduction. Introduce your Dalmatian at a distance and over time (weeks) allow it to come closer and closer to the baby. By introducing the baby slowly you are allowing your Dalmatian to know that it is worthy of its respect. Most dogs have no issues with new babies! However if you are not 100% confident with the safety of your baby I recommend rehoming your dog. The safety of your baby and dog are the greatest priority (dogs that attack a baby are normally euthanized)!

## Location

It is important to consider where you will be living with your new dog. If you are going to be living in a small apartment, or a house without a garden, it may be a good idea to consider purchasing a smaller breed of dog. Likewise, it is important to consider if you neighbors will be bothered by the sound of your dog barking. It may be worthwhile purchasing a breed that is known to be more silent! As a dog owner you will have to ensure that you and your dog have a suitable place to live.

## Dogs After a Death

Death is a natural part of life, but that does not make it any less painful. As previously mentioned, dogs have a unique ability to sooth people and empathize with them. This makes the purchase of a dog great for anyone who has experienced a death in their family. This is a piece of anecdotal evidence that I think emphasizes my point. After the death of my girlfriend's Granddad, her Grandmother was understandably distraught. She stopped going out as much and my girlfriend's family worried this could lead to illness. They decided to purchase her a Golden Retriever and I can safely say it has changed her life for the better. By owning a dog, it gave her a reason to get up in the morning, to get out of the house and it also gave her company in her home. Her Golden Retriever helped to ease the loneliness and sadness that comes after an impactful loss. If you, or someone in your family, has gone through a loss it may be worth considering getting a dog to help ease the pain. Another reason purchasing a dog from someone who has experienced a loss is the fact that people will talk to them while they are walking their dog. Dog owners get stopped and chatted to on a regular basis and this can definitely help ease the pain of a loss.

# The Death of a Dog

While this section is mainly applicable to families who have children, I think it is important for any dog owner to consider. When a dear family pet passes away it will always cause sadness and an 'emptiness' in a household. The best way to ease the pain of your pet's passing is to remove all of their bowls, dog beds and toys into an out of the way storage area. This will stop you, and your family, being constantly reminded by the absence. If you have small children it may be a good idea to purchase them a cuddly stuffed dog toy, of the same breed as your deceased dog. This can help to ease the transition period after the death. There is no right or wrong way to process the pain of a loss but there are definitely some things to avoid. If you are planning on introducing a new dog to your household it is important to not think of the new dog as a 'replacement.' To view a new animal as a replacement for an old animal is to disregard the individual personality of the new dog. Each dog is different in their own way and a new dog will not necessarily be interested in the activities, manner of petting and the food your previous dog enjoyed. The new dog may process affection differently and it may take time to adjust. I suggest not rushing into introducing a new dog into your family to avoid this.

# FINAL THOUGHTS

Thank you for purchasing our pet care manual on caring for a Dalmatian. I hope you have found the information both interesting and informative. I hope that this book has allowed you to make an informed choice on whether owning a Dalmatian suits you and if so I hope that the information will help you to provide the best quality care for your pet Dalmatian.

I will be publishing multiple other dog care manuals on our author page on Kindle. If you have an interest in learning more about specific dog breeds then I highly suggest you check out our other work.

I am passionate about providing the best quality information to our customers. I would highly appreciate any feedback, or reviews, you could leave us on our Kindle page to allow us to help create the best possible pet care products available on the market.

Made in the USA
Monee, IL
01 December 2022

19123040R00069